Let's Meet
Jackie Robinson

J
B
Robinson

"I'm not concerned with your liking or disliking me.
All I ask is that you respect me as a human being."
–Jackie Robinson

Helen Frost

CHELSEA CLUBHOUSE
An Imprint of Chelsea House Publishers
A Haights Cross Communications Company
Philadelphia

Chelsea Clubhouse books are published by Chelsea House Publishers, a subsidiary of Haights Cross Communications.

A Haights Cross Communications ⋆ Company

The Chelsea House World Wide Web address is www.chelseahouse.com

Printed and bound in the United States of America.

9 8 7 6 5 4 3 2 1

Library of Congress Cataloging-in-Publication Data
Frost, Helen, 1949–
    Let's meet Jackie Robinson / Helen Frost.
       p. cm. — (Let's meet biographies)
Summary: Simple text and photographs introduce the life of Jackie Robinson, the great African-American athlete who broke the color barrier in major league baseball during the 1940s.
Includes bibliographical references and index.
ISBN 0-7910-7321-1
1. Robinson, Jackie, 1919–1972—Juvenile literature. 2. Baseball players—United States—Biography—Juvenile literature. 3. African American baseball players—Biography—Juvenile literature. [1. Robinson, Jackie, 1919–1972. 2. Baseball players. 3. African Americans—Biography.] I. Title. II. Series.
GV865.R6F78 2004
796.357'092—dc21   2003004748

Editorial Credits

Lois Wallentine, editor; Takeshi Takahashi, designer; Mary Englar, photo researcher

Content Reviewer

James L. Gates Jr., Library Director, National Baseball Hall of Fame and Museum, Inc., Cooperstown, N.Y.

Photo Credits

Bettman/Corbis: cover, title page, 8, 11, 16, 20; Hulton Archive/Getty: 4, 5, 12; National Baseball Hall of Fame Library: 6-7, 13, 15, 18, 26; Pasadena Museum of History: 9; AP/Wide World: 10, 17, 21, 22, 24, 25, 27, 29; Library of Congress: 14, 19; Topps Company, Inc.: 23.

Table of Contents

Growing Up

Jackie Robinson was born on January 31, 1919. His family lived near Cairo, Georgia. His mother's name was Mallie and his father's name was Jerry.

Jackie was the youngest of five children.

Mrs. Robinson (seated) is surrounded by her children. From left to right are Mack, Jackie, Edgar, Willa Mae, and Frank.

When Jackie was a baby, his father went to look for a job. He did not come back.

In 1920, Mrs. Robinson moved the family to Pasadena, California. Jackie's mother worked hard as a housekeeper for other families.

Jackie stands with his classmates and teachers at Washington Junior High School in Pasadena.

Young Jackie played dodgeball and soccer. He liked to watch his brother Mack play baseball. When Jackie was 8 years old, his mother made him a ball out of old wool socks. He used a stick to practice hitting the ball.

Jackie was good at sports. Kids always wanted him on their team. Some kids offered to share their lunches with Jackie if he played on their team.

Jackie's family lived in a mostly white neighborhood. Some neighbors were **prejudiced.** They did not respect black people. They tried to make Jackie's family move.

Mrs. Robinson would not move. She taught her children **self-respect.** She taught them to be kind. But when people teased Jackie, he teased them back. He always stood up for himself.

Mack

The Robinson children earned respect through sports. Mack was a track star in college (below) and won a silver medal at the 1936 Olympics in Berlin, Germany.

Jackie went to John Muir Technical High School in Pasadena.

In high school, Jackie was a strong **athlete** in four sports. He played football, basketball, and baseball. He also ran track. His family was proud of him.

College and the Army

In 1937, Jackie started college in Pasadena. He starred in all four sports. After two years, Jackie went to the University of California in Los Angeles (called UCLA). He was an excellent player in all sports again.

Jackie poses in his UCLA basketball uniform. He was the first athlete at UCLA to earn a **letter** in four sports.

Jackie runs for extra yards after catching a pass for UCLA in this football game.

Sports were **integrated** at many colleges. Black athletes and white athletes played on the same teams. But most **professional** teams would not hire black players in the 1940s.

Jackie was a great athlete. Yet he knew the top professional teams would not hire him to play sports. In 1941, he quit college and started working. He wanted to help support his mother.

Jackie was drafted into the army during World War II. Here he trains with a rifle.

In 1942, Jackie was **drafted** into the U.S. Army. At this time, **segregation** was legal in some states. Laws kept blacks separate from whites. In the army, blacks and whites lived in separate areas. Blacks were not allowed in some restaurants on the army base.

Bus companies in southern states made blacks sit in the back seats. But on army bases, the rules said black soldiers could sit in any seat. One evening, Jackie boarded a bus on the base and sat near the front. The driver told Jackie to move to the back. Jackie did not move. He was arrested and had to go to court.

The judge said Jackie should be treated the same as white soldiers. Jackie won his case.

After Jackie won his case, he wanted to leave the army. He received an honorable **discharge.**

Playing Professional Baseball

In 1945, the Kansas City Monarchs hired Jackie. The Monarchs were an all-black baseball team.

Jackie played shortstop for the Kansas City Monarchs.

Jackie

Jackie's talent gave him a spot on the
Negro leagues' All-Star Team.

At this time, baseball was segregated by
leagues. Only whites could play on teams in the
major leagues. Blacks played on teams in the
Negro leagues.

Jackie agrees to play
baseball for Branch Rickey.

Branch Rickey was president of the Brooklyn
Dodgers major league team. He wanted great
athletes of all **races** to play in the major
leagues. He picked Jackie to play for the Dodgers.

Mr. Rickey knew some people would treat
Jackie badly. He asked Jackie if he could keep
from losing his temper.

All his life, Jackie had stood up for himself. He asked, "Mr. Rickey, are you looking for a Negro who is afraid to fight back?"

Mr. Rickey answered, "I'm looking for a ballplayer with guts enough not to fight back."

Jackie thought hard. He agreed to play for Mr. Rickey. He agreed not to show his anger.

Jackie's Family

Jackie met Rachel Isum at college in 1940. In 1946, Jackie and Rachel married. They had three children. This picture shows daughter Sharon, Jackie, Rachel, son David, and son Jackie Jr. celebrating Jackie's 35th birthday in 1954.

In 1946, Jackie joined Mr. Rickey's Montreal Royals minor league team. One year later, Jackie became a Brooklyn Dodger. On April 15, 1947, he became the first black athlete in more than 50 years to play in the major leagues.

Many people treated Jackie badly. Jackie was angry, but he didn't show it. He kept his promise to Mr. Rickey.

Jackie enters the locker room to trade his Montreal Royals uniform for a Brooklyn Dodgers uniform.

DODGERS CLUB HOUSE

KEEP OUT

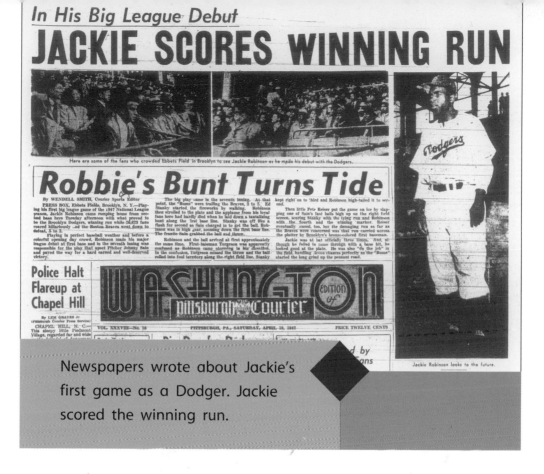

Newspapers wrote about Jackie's first game as a Dodger. Jackie scored the winning run.

Some Dodgers didn't want a black player on their team. Then they saw how well Jackie played. They came to respect him.

At one game, the other team yelled insults at Jackie. The Dodgers' team captain, Pee Wee Reese, put his hand on Jackie's shoulder. Pee Wee showed everyone his respect for Jackie.

Jackie accepts the Rookie of the Year award from sportswriter Jack Ryan.

That first season was hard. Jackie controlled his anger. He fought prejudice by being a great baseball player. Jackie made 12 homeruns. He stole more bases than any other player. Jackie was named **Rookie** of the Year.

Later, Jackie remembered that season. He wrote, "I started the season as a lonely man....
I ended it feeling like a member of a solid team. The Dodgers...had learned that it's not skin color but talent and ability that counts."

The 1947 lineup included third baseman Spider Jorgensen, shortstop Pee Wee Reese, second baseman Eddie Stanky, and first baseman Jackie Robinson.

Jackie's Honors

Jackie played for the Brooklyn Dodgers for 10 years. He made 137 home runs. He stole 197 bases. Baseball fans of all races loved and respected Jackie.

In 1948, Jackie started playing second base. He and shortstop Pee Wee Reese often worked together to get two runners out in a single play.

Jackie Robinson's Baseball Statistics

During Jackie's 10-year career with the Brooklyn Dodgers, he:

▶ Played 1,382 games

▶ Was up to bat 4,877 times

▶ Hit the ball and made it to base 1,518 times

▶ Scored 947 runs, including 137 home runs

▶ Struck out 291 times

▶ Played in six World Series

▶ Won the World Series in 1955

Jackie's 1956 baseball card

Jackie earned these honors:

▶ National League Rookie of the Year, 1947

▶ National League Most Valuable Player, 1949

▶ Named to six National League All-Star Teams

▶ Named to the National Baseball Hall of Fame, 1962

Jackie steals home during the first game of the 1955 World Series.

In 1955, the Dodgers won the World Series. They finally had baseball's top honor.

Two years later, Jackie **retired** from baseball. By then, many black baseball players were in the major leagues. Jackie's success had helped them.

After Jackie retired, he became vice president of a group of restaurants. He also spoke out for **civil rights**. He worked with **Martin Luther King Jr.** and other civil rights leaders. They wanted all people to be treated fairly.

Jackie helped black people fight for fair treatment and civil rights.

Jackie received many awards. In 1956, he was given the Spingarn Medal for his work for civil rights. In 1962, he was chosen to be in the National Baseball Hall of Fame. It was a great honor.

In June 1972, the Dodgers showed respect for Jackie by retiring his uniform number. The number 42 would no longer be used on any Dodgers uniform.

Jackie's family surrounds him after he received the National Baseball Hall of Fame award.

Rachel

Jackie Jr.

Jackie

mother-in-law, Zellee Isum

David

Sharon

"A LIFE IS NOT IMPORTANT EXCEPT IN THE IMPACT IT HAS ON OTHER LIVES."

Jackie Robinson

One of Jackie's sayings is carved in his tombstone. Jackie believed every person can make a difference.

Jackie died on October 24, 1972. In 1997, all major league teams honored Jackie by retiring number 42 from their baseball uniforms. Today, people still remember Jackie's skill in baseball and the courage he showed in fighting prejudice.

Important Dates in Jackie's Life

1919—Jackie is born on January 31 in Cairo, Georgia.

1920—Jackie moves with his family to Pasadena, California.

1937—Jackie goes to Pasadena Junior College.

1939—Jackie starts at the University of California—Los Angeles.

1942—Jackie is drafted into the U.S. Army.

1945—Jackie plays for the Kansas City Monarchs, a Negro league baseball team.

1946—Jackie marries Rachel Isum in February; he starts playing for the Montreal Royals minor league team in April; son Jackie Jr. is born in November.

1947—Jackie starts playing for the Brooklyn Dodgers; he is named National League Rookie of the Year.

1950—Daughter Sharon is born in January.

1952—Son David is born in May.

1955—Jackie helps the Brooklyn Dodgers win the World Series.

1957—Jackie retires from major league baseball.

1962—Jackie is named to the National Baseball Hall of Fame.

1972—Jackie dies on October 24 in Stamford, Connecticut; number 42 is retired by the Dodgers.

1984—Jackie is awarded the Presidential Medal of Freedom.

1997—Number 42 is retired by all major league teams.

More about the Negro Leagues

The first professional baseball league in the United States began in 1871. A few players were black, but most were white. Some team owners objected to the black players. In 1887, members of the International League had an agreement that blacks could not play in their league. This was the start of segregation in baseball.

Black players began organizing all-black teams in the 1880s. In the 1900s, they started the Negro leagues. Life was hard for Negro league players. They often traveled long distances to play other teams in the league. Restaurants and hotels in many places were segregated. Team members often had to eat and sleep on buses. Yet the athletes attracted crowds everywhere they played.

In the 1940s, many people wanted major league teams to integrate. They wanted black players to be recognized for their skills and treated fairly. Branch Rickey was one of those people. He was waiting for the right time and the right player.

Soon after Mr. Rickey signed Jackie Robinson to his team, several other major league

After Jackie became a Dodger, other Negro league players signed with major league teams. In this 1950 photo, Jackie stands with Larry Doby, Don Newcombe, Luke Easter, and Roy Campanella.

team owners started hiring black players, such as Larry Doby, "Satchel" Paige, "Hank" Aaron, and Willie Mays. Many black players later said that Jackie Robinson's success opened the door for them. He broke through the color barrier in baseball. The Negro leagues ended in the 1960s. Today, 40 percent of major league baseball players are minorities. People from all backgrounds now play professional sports.

Glossary

athlete—someone who plays sports

civil rights—the rights that all people in a country have; everyone has the right to freedom and equal treatment under the law; Jackie joined picket lines and raised money to help black people win their civil rights.

discharge—to let go officially

drafted—made to join; during World War II (1939-1945), the government needed soldiers to fight; many young men were drafted into the army.

integrate—to include people of all races; major league baseball was integrated when Jackie became a Dodger.

league—a group of sports teams that compete with each other

letter—a patch with the school's initials that athletes earn for success in a sport; athletes sometimes put the letter patches on their school jackets.

Martin Luther King Jr.—a minister who led the civil rights movement in the 1950s and 1960s by using peaceful ways to challenge unfair laws

prejudice—an unfair opinion about someone based on the person's race, religion, or other characteristic

professional—to earn money for working or performing

race—a large group of people that share the same physical features, such as skin color; the features are passed from one generation to the next.

retire—to give up work, usually because of your age or ability to do the work; also to stop using something; all major league teams retired Jackie's number in 1997.

rookie—a player in his or her first year; a "Rookie of the Year" is the best first-year player in a sport.

segregation—the act of keeping people or groups apart; before the 1960s, blacks and whites in many parts of the United States were kept separate; today, segregation is illegal in the United States.

self-respect—pride in yourself; the feeling that you have value

To Learn More

▶ **Read these books about Jackie:**

Adler, David A. *A Picture Book of Jackie Robinson*. New York: Holiday House, 1994.

Golenbock, Peter. *Teammates*. San Diego: Harcourt Brace Jovanovich, 1990.

Klingel, Cynthia Fitterer and Robert B. Noyed. *Jackie Robinson*. Level Two: Wonder Books. Chanhassen, Minn.: Child's World, 2001.

Schaefer, Lola M. *Jackie Robinson*. First Biographies. Mankato, Minn.: Pebble Books, 2003.

▶ **Look up these web sites:**

Los Angeles Dodgers' History: Jackie Robinson Time Line

www.dodgers.com/NASApp/mlb/la/history/jackie_robinson_timeline/
timeline_index.jsp
View video clips, see pictures, and follow a time line of Jackie's life.

The National Baseball Hall of Fame: Primary Sources—Jackie Robinson

www.baseballhalloffame.org/education/primary_sources/robinson_jackie/
index.htm
See Jackie's Hall of Fame biography and plaque. Also, search for Branch Rickey's Hall of Fame biography and plaque.

Jackie Robinson Foundation: About Jackie

www.jackierobinson.org/aboutjackie/index.html
Learn more about Jackie's life on this web site for a scholarship foundation started by Jackie's wife, Rachel Robinson.

▶ **Key Internet search terms:**

Jackie Robinson, Negro leagues, Dodgers history, Branch Rickey

Index

Oct. 2003